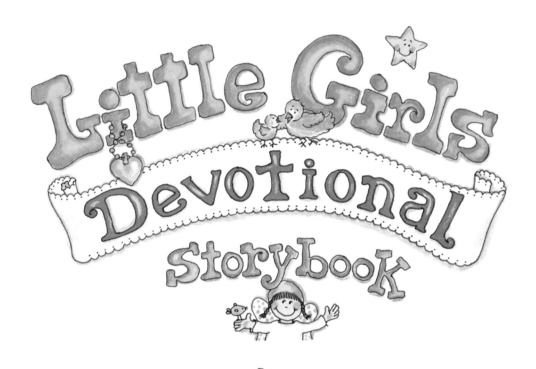

Little Girls Devotional Storybook

for Mothers ♥ Daughters

Little Girls Devotional Storybook for Mothers & Daughters

Copyright © 2000 Baker Book House Company, Grand Rapids, Michigan.

New Kids Media™ is published by Baker Book House Company, Grand Rapids, Michigan.

ISBN 0-8010-4446-4

Printed in the United States of America.

1 2 3 4 5 6 7 — 03 02 01 00

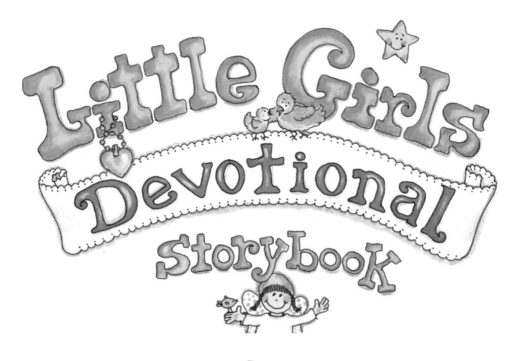

Little Girls Devotional Storybook

for Mothers  Daughters

Carolyn Larsen

Illustrated by Caron Turk

NEW Kids MEDiA

BAKER
A DIVISION OF
Baker Book House Co

Presented to:

ASHLEY & KRISTINA

Date:

12-25-00

Table of Contents

Maggie Disobeys 8

The Thank-You Week 18

Two Simple Words 28

Try, Try Again 38

I Don't Know 48

The Scary Night 58

Mommy's Special Helper 68

Just Like Me! 78

God's Special Care 88

You've Got Thomas! 98

Taking What's Not Mine 108

All For Me! 118

The Best Birthday Gift 128

The Best Me I Can Be 138

Prayers for Tammy 148

My Mom 158

The Broken Lamp 168

The Right-Now Girl 178

Maggie Disobeys

"Can I go to Kara's house?" Maggie asked. "Please, Mommy. Please, please, pretty please with sugar on it?" Maggie's big blue eyes begged her mommy to say yes.

"I don't have time to walk with you, and, it's too far for you to go by yourself," Mommy said. Maggie's bottom lip stuck right out in a big pout. "Why don't you play with Lindsay next door?" Mommy continued.

Maggie didn't want to play with Lindsay. She wanted to play with Kara. Just then Maggie had an idea. She ran to the big bushes at the edge of Lindsay's yard. Dropping down on her tummy, Maggie scooted between them.

Maggie ran all the way to Kara's house, even though Mommy had said not to go there. Maggie and Kara played in the sandbox and slid down the slide. They had a tea party with all of Kara's dolls.

Pretty soon Mommy went to Lindsay's house to bring Maggie home. But Maggie wasn't there! Mommy looked in the backyard, but Maggie wasn't there. She looked in Maggie's room—no Maggie. Where could Maggie be?

"I know Maggie wanted to play at Kara's house," thought Mommy, "surely she wouldn't go there by herself." But, when Mommy went to Kara's house, there was Maggie with a dress-up hat covering her bouncy curls.

Mommy didn't say anything all the way home. Maggie ran her bedroom and curled up with her soft pink teddy bear. Big teardrops trickled down her face. She felt bad that she had disobeyed Mommy.

Later, Mommy came in and snuggled by Maggie. "I said you couldn't go to Kara's because it's not safe for you to go that far by yourself."

"I know," Maggie sniffled, "I'm sorry I didn't obey."

Mommy kissed the top of Maggie's curly head, "I forgive you, Honey, and I love you forever!"

Maggie Disobeys

1. How did Maggie disobey?
2. Was Maggie sorry for disobeying? How do you know?
3. What did Mommy do after Maggie said she was sorry?
4. When was a time you disobeyed? How did you feel afterwards?

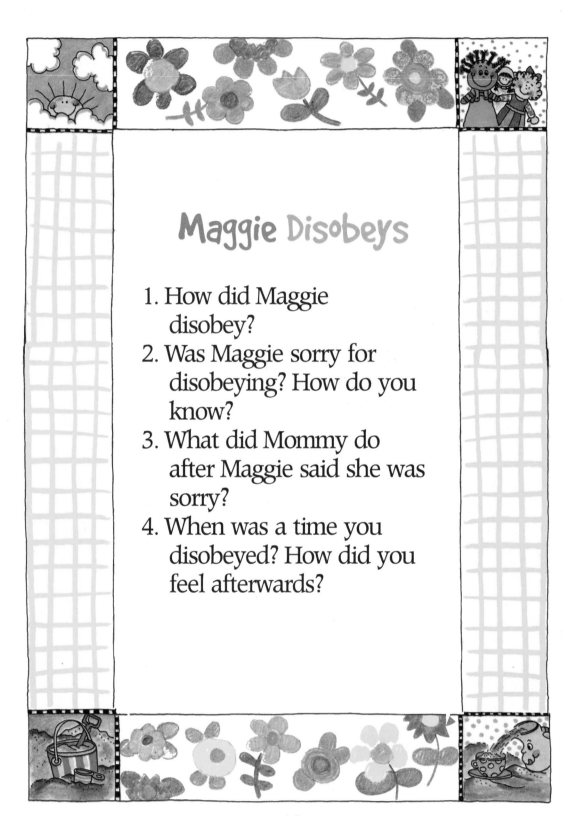

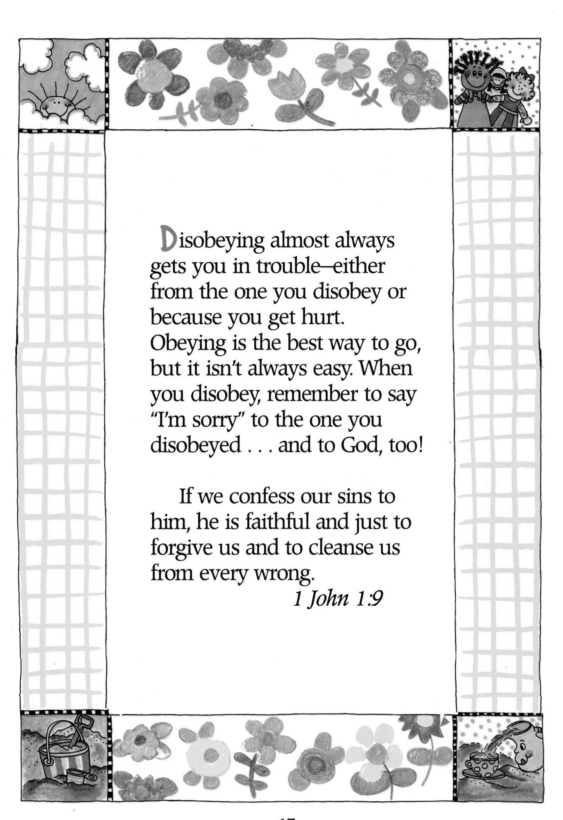

Disobeying almost always gets you in trouble—either from the one you disobey or because you get hurt. Obeying is the best way to go, but it isn't always easy. When you disobey, remember to say "I'm sorry" to the one you disobeyed . . . and to God, too!

If we confess our sins to him, he is faithful and just to forgive us and to cleanse us from every wrong.

1 John 1:9

The Thank-You Week

"Let's have a Thank-You Week," suggested Mom.
"What's that?" asked Sarah.

"Each day we'll think of one thing to thank God for,"
Mom explained. Sarah thought that was a good idea.
She got her paper and markers and made a big sign that
read Sarah's Thank-You Week!

On Monday Sarah wrote, Thank You for Mommy, who gives me hugs and kisses. She reads to me and sings to me and makes yummy dinners! I love Mommy!

Tuesday Sarah drew a picture of Daddy crawling on hands and knees—giving her a horseback ride. Thank you for Daddy, the sign read. He plays with me and tickles me and helps me with my good night prayers. I love Daddy!

On Wednesday Sarah added, Thank you for my friends. We have so much fun together because we all like to play dolls and have tea parties. We share special secrets and giggle and laugh. I love my friends!

Thursday's special thank you was for pets:
Thank you for my puppy that snuggles with
me when I'm sad or makes me laugh when she
plays with a bug.

I love my church, Sarah wrote on Friday. Thank you for Pastor Dave and for my Sunday school teachers. I like to sing songs about you and learn verses from the Bible.

On Saturday, Sarah thought and thought. It was getting harder to think of things she was thankful for. Finally she wrote, Thank You for my home. It's warm and safe and I have a pretty bedroom with a pink ruffled bed.

Sunday morning Sarah knew right away what to write: I'm really thankful for all the things on my Thank You Week list, but most of all I'm thankful for . . . You! Thank You God for You!

The Thank-You Week

1. What things was Sarah thankful for that you are also thankful for?
2. Who are some people you are thankful for?
3. Do you usually remember to say "thank you" to other people and to God?
4. When have you done something for someone and that person thanked you? How did you feel?

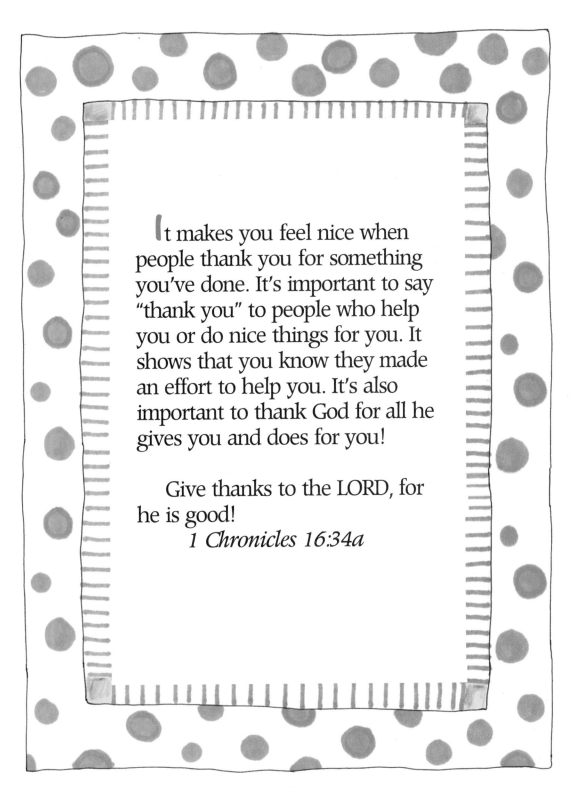

It makes you feel nice when people thank you for something you've done. It's important to say "thank you" to people who help you or do nice things for you. It shows that you know they made an effort to help you. It's also important to thank God for all he gives you and does for you!

Give thanks to the LORD, for he is good!
1 Chronicles 16:34a

Two Simple Words

Mallory did happy somersaults all around the house. She and Mommy were going to Aunt Vicki's! Mommy and Aunt Vicki were good friends, and Mallory and Jason, Aunt Vicki's son, were friends, too! It was going to be a fun day!

Their mommies drank iced tea and talked while Mallory and Jason splashed in the wading pool and made mud pies in the corner of Aunt Vicki's garden. She even let them pick juicy, red tomatoes from the big, green tomato plants.

Mallory and Jason sat in the shade
drinking cold lemonade, telling funny stories
and making silly noises. But then . . . "It's time
to go home!" Mommy called.

"Not yet! We're going to play school and
I'm the teacher!" Mallory whined.

"You'll have to save that for next visit,"
Mommy said. "We need to go home!"

Mallory's face froze in an angry pout as she picked up toys. "Oh, I nearly forgot—I have something for you, Mallory," said Aunt Vicki. She held out a shiny hair barrette with "Mallory" written in pink glitter paint across the top and a pink bow hanging down. (Pink was Mallory's favorite color!)

Mallory really liked the barrette, and she knew that she should say "Thank you" to Aunt Vicki. But she didn't. She was too busy being mad because she had to go home. She just crossed her arms and stuck her bottom lip out in the biggest pout she had ever pouted.

"What do you say?" Mommy gently reminded. But Mallory turned away and wouldn't say a word. Mommy kept asking, "Mallory, what do you say?" and Aunt Vicki kept saying, "It's OK, really it is." (But it wasn't OK, deep down inside Mallory knew that.)

Jason stood by watching the whole thing. Suddenly, he knew exactly what to do! With two fingers he grabbed Mallory's top lip, with the other hand he gently took her bottom lip. Then he moved them open and closed, just like a puppet while he squeaked in a funny voice, "Thank you!"

Mommy laughed. Aunt Vicki laughed. Mallory was so surprised that she laughed, too! When it was finally quiet, Mallory said, "I'm sorry, Aunt Vicki. Thank you for the barrette, it's pretty."

"And," Mommy added, "Thank you, Jason for helping Mallory say, "Thank you!"

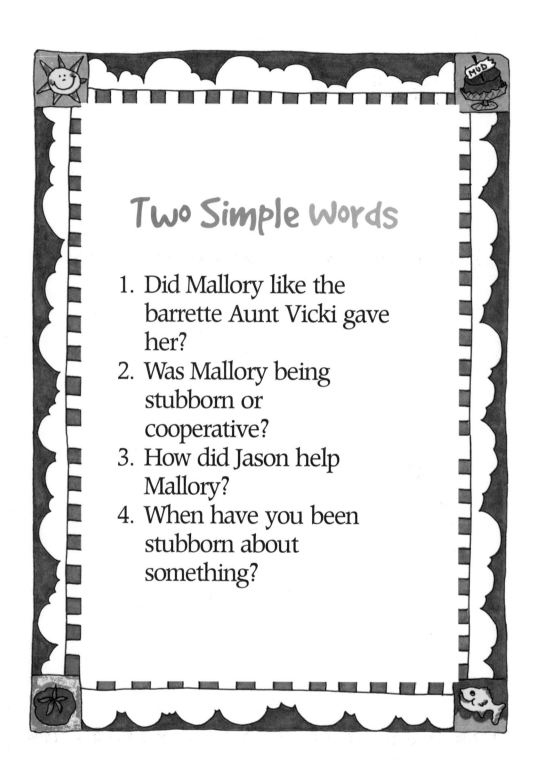

Two Simple Words

1. Did Mallory like the barrette Aunt Vicki gave her?
2. Was Mallory being stubborn or cooperative?
3. How did Jason help Mallory?
4. When have you been stubborn about something?

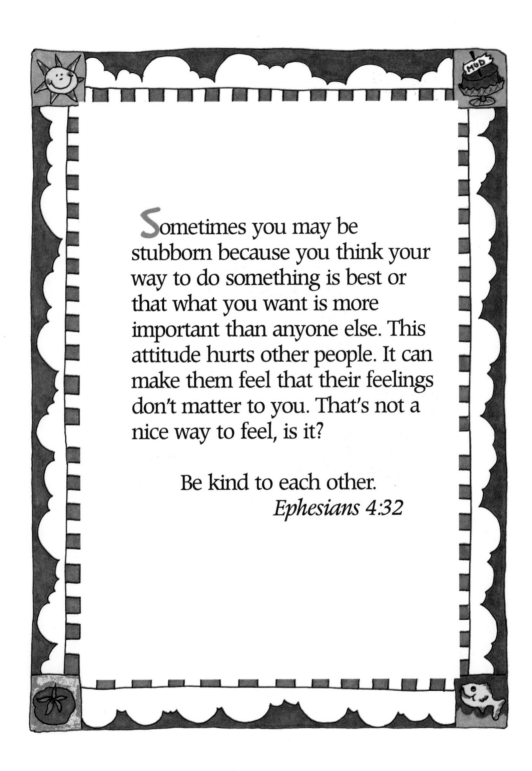

Sometimes you may be stubborn because you think your way to do something is best or that what you want is more important than anyone else. This attitude hurts other people. It can make them feel that their feelings don't matter to you. That's not a nice way to feel, is it?

Be kind to each other.
Ephesians 4:32

Try, Try Again!

One day, out of the clear blue sky, Lauren said, "Can I play softball? Jill is on the park district team and she has lots of fun."

"I used to play," Mommy said. "I can teach you how." So, Mommy and Lauren went shopping for a new, leather softball glove and a shiny, white softball (which really wasn't very soft at all).

Mommy found her old glove in the basement and they went out to play catch. Mommy gently tossed the softball to Lauren. Lauren held her glove up to catch it, but the ball sailed right by. "Watch the ball very closely," Mommy called.

Mommy took a step closer to Lauren and
threw the ball a little lower. Lauren squished
her tongue between her lips and tried so hard
to catch it, but she wasn't even close. "Watch
it all the way into your glove," Mommy called.

For a whole hour Mommy tossed the ball to Lauren. Lauren didn't catch it even once. Each time she chased after the ball and threw it back to Mommy—sometimes she even got it close to where Mommy was standing!

"How about a lemonade break?" Mommy suggested. (She looked a little more tired than Lauren). After a few minutes Lauren was bouncing around the yard.

"Throw the ball some more, Mommy, I'll catch it this time!"

Mommy threw the ball right at Lauren's glove . . .
and it landed under the prickly rose bush. Next time,
it landed in the sand box. Each time, Lauren picked
up the ball and smacked it in her glove a few times—
just like the ball players on TV did.

"Last toss, Lauren. I have to make dinner," Mommy called. Lauren's forehead wrinkled in concentration. She locked her eyes on the ball and held her glove up high. SMACK! The ball landed right in the middle of her glove.

"I caught it! I did!" Lauren hopped and jumped and shouted. "I did it! I did it!"

Mommy swept Lauren into her arms and twirled her around in a great big circle! "I'm so proud of you! You didn't give up—you kept trying and trying until you caught the ball! Yahoo for you!!"

Try, Try Again!

1. How many times did Lauren try to catch the ball before she gave up?
2. What did Mommy say to Lauren when she did catch the ball?
3. How do you feel when you have something hard to do?
4. When have you tried and tried to do something?

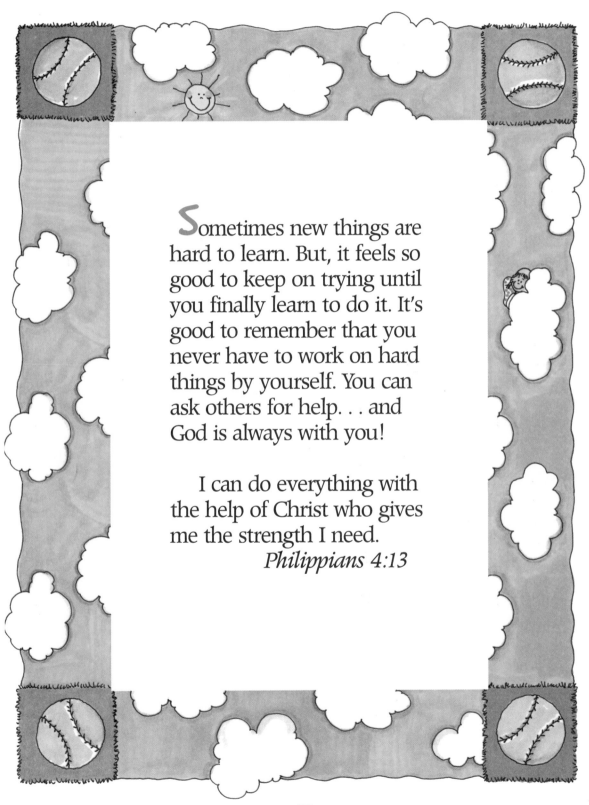

Sometimes new things are hard to learn. But, it feels so good to keep on trying until you finally learn to do it. It's good to remember that you never have to work on hard things by yourself. You can ask others for help. . . and God is always with you!

I can do everything with the help of Christ who gives me the strength I need.
Philippians 4:13

I Don't Know

"Who left this pile of books on the floor?"
Mommy asked.

Emily looked up from the picture she was
coloring and said, "I don't know."

"Who left the colors and coloring book in the middle of the floor?" Mommy asked.

Emily peeked out from around the doll house and said, "I don't know."

"Who forgot to put the doll house and
dolls back in the closet?" Mommy asked.
   Emily pulled up the hat she was trying on
and said, "I don't know."

"I wonder who left the dress-up clothes scattered here on the floor?" Mommy wondered.

Emily put another piece in the puzzle before she said, "I don't know."

"Oh dear, the puzzle pieces are still all over the floor. Who do you think forgot to put them back in the box?" Mommy asked softly.

Emily kept stacking blocks one on top of the other. "I don't know," she said, without even looking up.

"Hmmm," Mommy said, looking around at all the messes, "This 'I don't know' is a pretty messy person, isn't she?" But, Emily didn't say a word.

This little person really made a mess....

Mommy disappeared and came back in a few minutes with a big plate of chocolate chip cookies and a glass of cold milk. "Who is that for?" Emily asked—she could already taste the warm cookies."

"It's for 'I don't know,'" Mommy said. "I want to have a talk with her about picking up her toys and I thought it would be good over a snack."

"There isn't anyone here named 'I don't know'" Emily giggled. "It was me who left my toys out on the floor."

"Well, what do you know," Mommy smiled.

I Don't Know

1. Who left the toys and books out on the floor?
2. Why didn't Emily tell Mommy she did it?
3. Did Mommy know it was Emily's things on the floor?
4. Do you always pick up the things you get out?

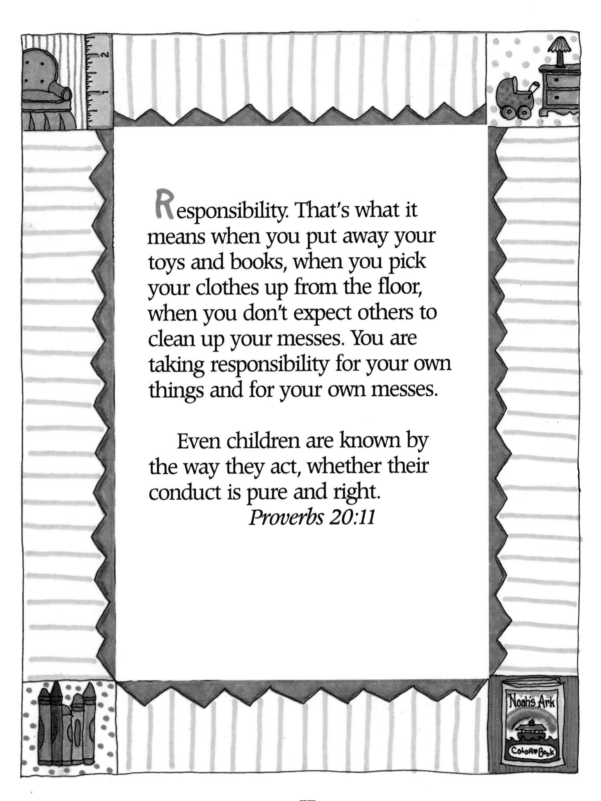

Responsibility. That's what it means when you put away your toys and books, when you pick your clothes up from the floor, when you don't expect others to clean up your messes. You are taking responsibility for your own things and for your own messes.

Even children are known by the way they act, whether their conduct is pure and right.
Proverbs 20:11

The Scary Night

Cori climbed into bed and tucked her teddy bear in next to her on one side and her favorite stuffed dolphin on the other side. She pulled the covers up under her chin and called, "Mommy, I'm ready for my good-night prayer."

Mommy sat down on the side of Cori's bed. "What do you want to thank God for tonight?"

"Um, for my friends and for you and Daddy and for Dexter my dolphin," said Cori, giving Dexter a big hug.

"Lights Out"

They finished praying and Mommy said, "Sleep tight, my love. See you in the morning." She gave Cori a big hug and turned out the light.

Cori snuggled down in her pillow and closed her eyes. Suddenly, a crash of thunder made her jump right out of bed. Dexter tumbled to the floor and pillows fell on top of him. Lightning flashed in the sky like cameras snapping a thousand pictures.

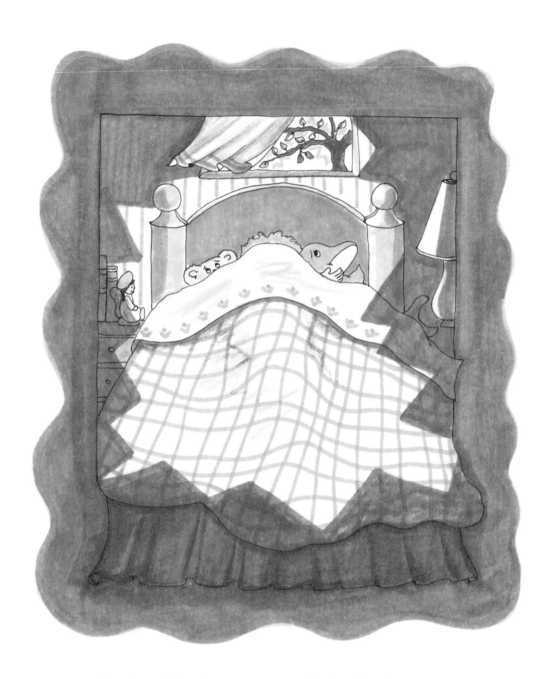

Cori grabbed Dexter and climbed back in bed, squeezing her eyes closed. Thunder crashed and banged and lightning zigzagged through the sky and Cori pulled the blankets over her head.

When she lifted the covers for a breath of fresh air, there were scary shadows crawling along her bedroom walls—like monsters walking around her room, lightning flashed and the tree outside her window was shaking and blowing angry branches around the sky.

"Mommy! Mommy!" Cori cried over the noise of
the storm. "I'm scared!"

Mommy snuggled in beside Cori and gently
stroked her back. "It's OK. There's nothing to be
scared of. Storms like this show us how much power
God has."

"I wish he would save some power for later," Cori whispered. "Can I sleep in your room?"

"Sure," Mommy smiled. So, Cori settled down in her sleeping bag right next to Mommy's bed with her teddy bear and Dexter snuggled in, too. Mommy reached her hand over the side and Cori fell asleep holding on to it.

The Scary Night

1. What was Cori afraid of?
2. Why did Cori feel better when she was with Mommy?
3. What are you afraid of?
4. What makes you feel less afraid?

"Lights Out"

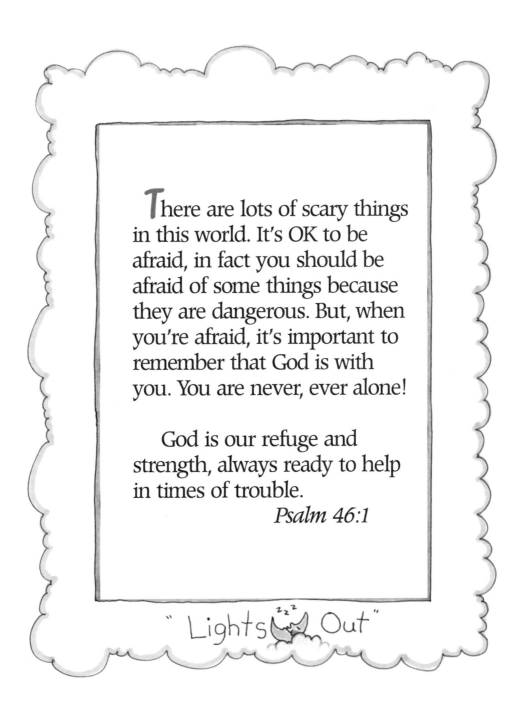

*T*here are lots of scary things in this world. It's OK to be afraid, in fact you should be afraid of some things because they are dangerous. But, when you're afraid, it's important to remember that God is with you. You are never, ever alone!

God is our refuge and strength, always ready to help in times of trouble.

Psalm 46:1

" Lights Out "

Mommy's Special Helper

"Look at all these dirty dishes," Mommy said.
"I wonder who could help me wash them?"

Mommy looked all around the room—high and low, but she pretended not to notice Samantha raising her hand and calling, "I can! I'll help!"

"Look at this dusty furniture. Why, I can write
my name in the dust," Mommy said. "I wonder
who could help me dust it?"

"I will, I will," Samantha shouted. But, Mommy wrote words in the dust and pretended not to hear.

"My, look at all the laundry that needs to be folded," Mommy said. "I wonder who could help me with these big towels and sheets?"

"Me, me! Mommy, I will be your helper," Samantha jumped up and down, waving her arms. But Mommy pretended not to see.

Samantha stood on a chair and took
Mommy's face in both her hands. "Mommy,
I will be your helper. I can help with all the
chores you have to do."

"Why, Samantha, are you saying that you would like to be my helper?" Mommy asked. When Samantha nodded yes Mommy said, "That makes me very happy. You will be the very best helper ever!"

Mommy's Special Helper

1. What things did Mommy need help with?
2. Who wanted to be Mommy's helper?
3. What are some ways you help your Mommy?
4. Does Mommy like it when you help her?

Grown-ups have a lot of work to do—taking care of the house, lawn, and cars. They appreciate any help you give. Helping shows that you care about them. Plus, when the work is done, they have time to spend with you!

Two people can accomplish more than twice as much as one; they get a better reward for their labor.

Ecclesiastes 4:9

Just Like Me!

"How was school today?" Mommy asked.
Kallie sighed her biggest six-year-old sigh
and said, "Not so very good. We didn't get to
go outside and play at recess."

"Mrs. Brown thought we should play inside games today . . . because of the new girl, Wendy. She sits in a wheelchair all the time. I think outside games are more fun," Kallie said softly.

The next day Kallie's class did go outside to play. Kallie played on the swings and went down the slide really fast and played tag with her friends.

A few times Kallie noticed Wendy sitting in her wheelchair in the shade by the building. No one talked to her or anything. She just sat and watched the rest of the kids having fun on the playground.

The next day Kallie was racing to the playground when she bumped Wendy's chair and the book on Wendy's lap fell to the ground. When she picked it up, Kallie noticed that it was about art. "Do you like to draw?" she asked, before she even thought about it.

"Kind of," Wendy said shyly.

Kallie played for a while, but kept watching Wendy reading her big art book. Finally, Kallie went over to her and said, "I like to draw pictures of my cat, Rascal."

"I have a cat, too," Wendy said softly. "Her name is Midnight."

Pretty soon Wendy and Kallie were talking
like old friends. They found out that they
both liked art and cats and chocolate chip
cookies. They both didn't like cooked carrots
or going to bed early.

The next recess, Kallie's friends called to her, "Come on, let's play tag!"

"Uhh, maybe later. I'm going to talk to Wendy for a while," Kallie answered. When the bell rang ending recess, Kallie and Wendy were still laughing and talking and drawing funny pictures of Rascal and Midnight.

Just Like Me!

1. Why did Kallie's class sometimes stay inside?
2. Do you think Wendy was lonely?
3. How was Kallie a friend to Wendy?
4. Who could you be a friend to?

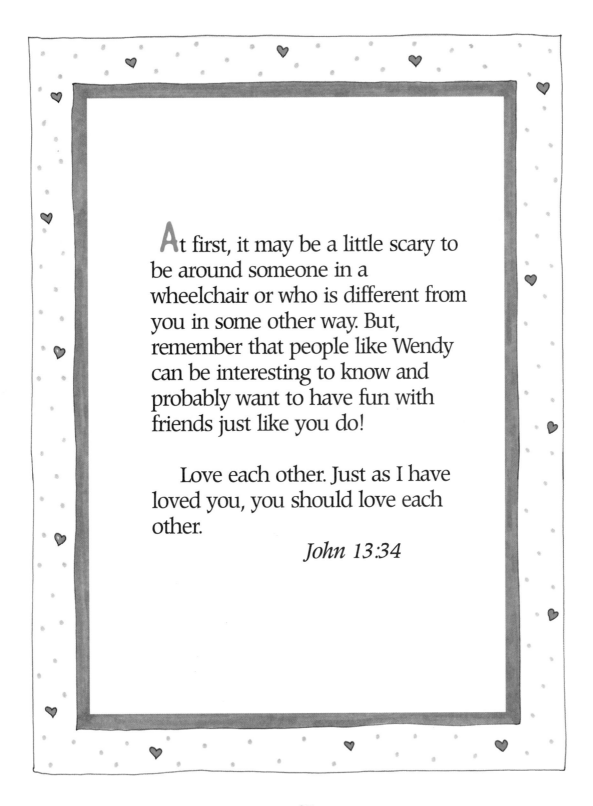

At first, it may be a little scary to be around someone in a wheelchair or who is different from you in some other way. But, remember that people like Wendy can be interesting to know and probably want to have fun with friends just like you do!

Love each other. Just as I have loved you, you should love each other.

John 13:34

God's Special care

"Momma, look what I found!" Shannon waved a bright blue feather back and forth. "Some bird outside is losing its clothes!"

"Who knows how many feathers a bird has?" Momma asked.

"I don't know," Shannon couldn't even guess.

"God knows," said Momma, swinging Shannon around the room.

"Who tells the birds when it'is time to go south for the winter?" Momma asked.

"Hmmmm," Shannon thought very hard.

"God does!" Momma cried.

"Who teaches birds how to make nests?"
Momma wondered, tickling Shannon's tummy.
"God does!" Shannon shouted.

"Who keeps eggs in the nest when the wind
blows and blows?" Shannon asked her
momma.

"God does!" Momma sang it like a song.

"I wonder who teaches birds how to fly and soar through the sky?" Momma tapped her chin and pretended to think very hard.

"God does!" Shannon giggled.

"I wonder who helps birds find worms hiding in the ground?" Shannon held out her hands in wonder.

"God does!" Momma grabbed her hands and they danced around the room.

"Who loves Shannon even more than he loves the birds?" Momma wondered aloud.

"God does!" Momma and Shannon shouted together.

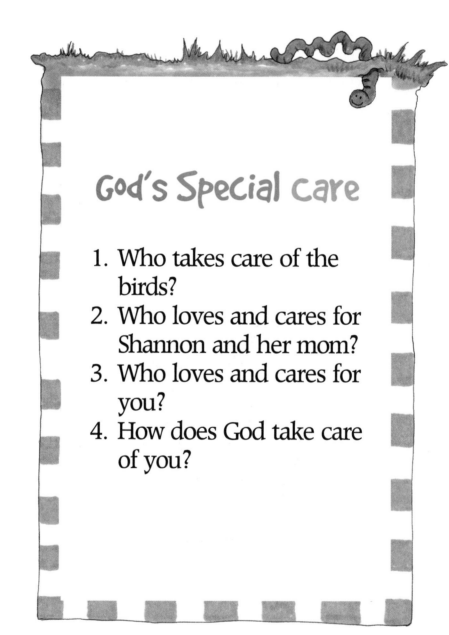

God's Special Care

1. Who takes care of the birds?
2. Who loves and cares for Shannon and her mom?
3. Who loves and cares for you?
4. How does God take care of you?

*T*ake a minute and think about all the wonderful ways God cares for you and the things he does for you. Many things you may take for granted—you expect the sun to come up every day and to see flowers in spring. Take a minute right now to thank him for all he does.

I will be your God throughout your lifetime . . . I made you and I will care for you.

Isaiah 46:4

You've Got Thomas!!!!

Momma heard the door slam and footsteps pounding up the stairs. "Gotta wash my hands!" Lindsey cried. "I've got Thomas on them!"

"How do you get that?" Momma asked.

"Teacher made me stand by Tina Thomas in chorus. No one likes her, so if you accidentally touch her—even her clothes—then you've got Thomas!" Lindsey explained.

"Oh, I see," Momma said (though she really didn't). "Then, what do you do?"

"Well, I have to tag someone else to give Thomas to them–then I don't have it anymore," said Lindsey. Soap bubbles floated away as she scrubbed her hands.

"Why don't you and your friends like Tina?"

"Oh, cause she doesn't wear clothes like ours—hers don't even fit her good and she doesn't have stuff like we have," Lindsey answered.

"At recess we always play Thomas Tag," she continued.

"What does Tina do while you play this tag?"

"I don't know. I guess she just laughs and watches us," Lindsey had never really thought about it.

"When you play other games does Tina play with you?" Momma wondered.

"Eeewww, no. No one wants to play with her!" Lindsey wrinkled her mouth into a not-very-pretty face.

We don't make fun of her....

"Hmmm, I wonder how Tina really feels when you guys are making fun of her," Momma said softly.

"We don't make fun of her," Lindsey defended herself and her friends.

No one said anything for awhile. Finally
Lindsey said, "Probably even if Tina is
laughing, her heart is sad about how we treat
her, huh?"

"Probably," Momma said.

"I think I'll tell her I'm sorry," Lindsey said.
Momma gave Lindsey a big hug as a tear
leaked down her cheek.

You've Got Thomas!

1. Why didn't kids like Tina?
2. How do you think Tina felt about "Thomas Tag"?
3. When was a time you were unkind to someone?
4. How do you feel now about the way you treated that person?

Of course Tina was lonely and hurt by the way the other kids treated her. You should always be kind to other people—being kind shows them God's love. Remember to treat other people the way you would like to be treated.

Do for others what you would like them to do for you.

Matthew 7:12

Taking What's Not Mine

"Momma, can I go to Jillian's house? I have so much fun at her house. She has the best dress-up clothes!" Julia folded her hands together and begged her mom to say yes.

Momma made a quick phone call to get permission from Jillian's mom, then walked Julia over to her house. Before long Jillian and Julia were pulling dress-up clothes from a big trunk.

Julia put on a frilly long pink dress that Jillian's mom had once worn in a wedding. She plopped a floppy pink hat on her blond curls—and her very favorite thing—a sparkly necklace with dark blue stones tucked between pretend diamonds. Julia just knew she looked beautiful.

The girls played all afternoon. They changed dresses, and wore different hats. But no matter what clothes Julia had on, she always wore the pretty blue and white sparkly necklace.

When it was time to go home, Julia helped Jillian put
the dress-up clothes back in the trunk. She took off
the necklace to put in the box where Jillian kept her
dress-up jewelry. Julia looked at the necklace—it was so
pretty. Suddenly she slipped the necklace into her
pocket, put the jewelry box back in the trunk and
closed the lid.

Julia didn't mean to steal the necklace from her friend. She just knew that she liked it so much that she wanted it to be hers. But walking home with her mom, it felt like her pocket was on fire! It felt like everyone could see the necklace in her pocket.

That night Julia couldn't sleep. She couldn't think about anything except the necklace. Julia felt terrible that she had stolen something from her friend. "Jillian probably won't want to be my friend anymore," she thought.

Early the next morning Julia went to her mom and told her the whole story. Momma listened quietly, then gave Julia a big hug. "Thank you for telling me. Now, let's go talk to Jillian together," Mom said.

Taking What's Not Mine

1. Why did Julia take the necklace?
2. How do you think Jillian felt when she discovered the necklace was gone?
3. Have you ever stolen something or been tempted to?
4. Why is it wrong to take something that doesn't belong to you?

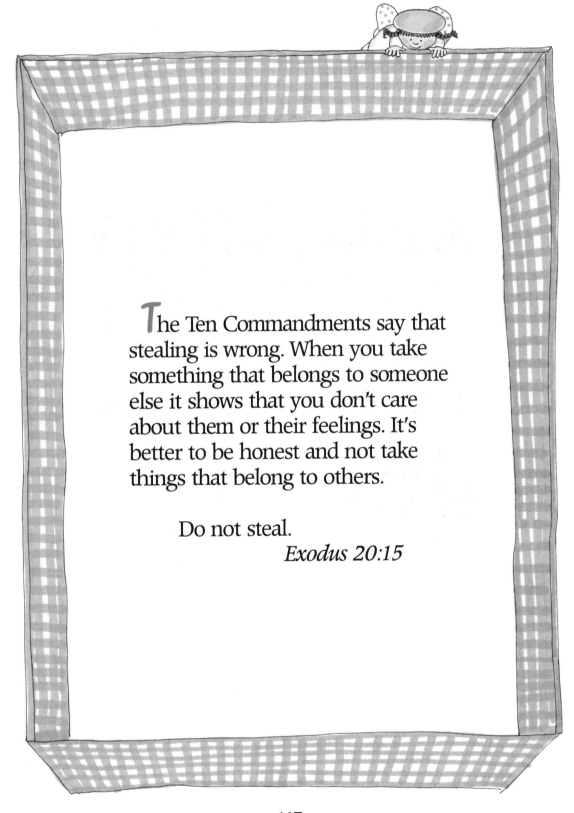

The Ten Commandments say that stealing is wrong. When you take something that belongs to someone else it shows that you don't care about them or their feelings. It's better to be honest and not take things that belong to others.

Do not steal.

Exodus 20:15

All For Me!

Cassie had a great plan! She was going to the movies with her friends. And . . . she had a great plan. They crowded around the candy counter and Mom said, "You can each get one thing." Cassie chose a box of tiny jawbreakers.

Cassie noticed that the others got chocolate bars or jelly beans or other yummy things. As soon as they settled down in the dark theater everyone opened their candies and started munching . . . except Cassie . . . she had a plan.

Cassie put one jawbreaker in her mouth and rolled it around, side to side, up and down. It lasted for a long time. By the time she was enjoying her third jawbreaker, everyone else's candy was gone. Cassie's plan was working!

When the movie was only half over the other kids started begging Cassie for a piece of her candy. But, she wouldn't share—she had a plan, you know—Cassie's great plan was to have lots of candy left when everyone else's was gone. Then everyone would be jealous of her!

Yum Yummy

Good

Yum

Soooooo

Yummy Yum

So, while everyone watched her instead of the movie, Cassie made a big show of putting a jawbreaker in her mouth and rolling it around. She even opened her mouth so the others could see how good her candy looked! "Can I have a piece," Cassie's very best friend, Sada asked. But, she wouldn't share, not even one piece!

By the time the movie was over, everyone was pretty mad at Cassie. But, she didn't care. "What a great plan I had," she thought as she stood up to leave the theater. But, then . . .

Cassie's hand bumped against the seat in front of her
   . . . and she dropped the box of tiny jawbreakers.
Blue, green, red, and yellow jawbreakers tumbled
under the rows and rows of seats–all the way to the
front of the theater.

"My candy!" Cassie cried, bursting into tears. Each of her friends secretly hid a smile and scooted past her–except Sada. Sada gently put her arm around Cassie's shoulder and said, "Too bad, Cassie. I'm sorry." And you know what . . . she really was!

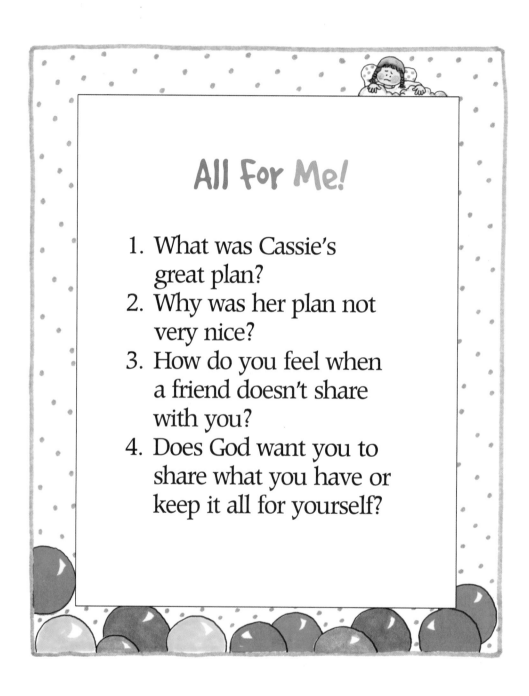

All for Me!

1. What was Cassie's great plan?
2. Why was her plan not very nice?
3. How do you feel when a friend doesn't share with you?
4. Does God want you to share what you have or keep it all for yourself?

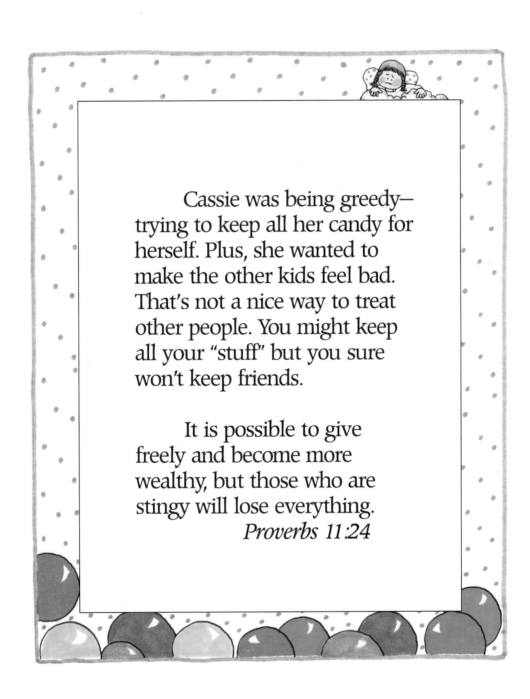

Cassie was being greedy—trying to keep all her candy for herself. Plus, she wanted to make the other kids feel bad. That's not a nice way to treat other people. You might keep all your "stuff" but you sure won't keep friends.

It is possible to give freely and become more wealthy, but those who are stingy will lose everything.
Proverbs 11:24

The Best Birthday Gift

"Happy birthday to me, in ten days!" Jessie sang. "Just in case you forgot, I made a What-I-Want-for-My-Birthday List," she announced and she handed a paper to Grandma.

"My, you have a very long wish list." Grandma counted twenty things on Jessie's paper. "Which thing do you really want the most?"

"Oh, I want all of them—everything on the list," Jessie answered.

My Birthday Wish List...

1. VIDEOS
2. Doll
3. Books
4. MUSIC CD's
5. Jewelry
6. New Bike

Yummy

"Afternoon, Mildred," a voice from the sidewalk called. Jessie looked up to see a bent over old man wearing a jacket that was probably worn out 10 years ago.

"Who is that?" Jessie asked with a little disgust in her voice. "Yuck, why doesn't he get a new coat?"

"That's Mr. Smith from down the block," Grandma answered. "I doubt if he can afford a new coat. A social security check doesn't stretch too far with today's prices." Jessie watched the old man shuffle down the street. He looked lonely.

But, Jessie quickly forgot about Mr. Smith and
hurried back to explaining her birthday list to
Grandma. She wanted to be sure Grandma
knew exactly which video game to get and
what color hair the baby doll should have.

The next morning Jessie helped Grandma plant flowers near the sidewalk. She was digging up cool black soil when a ripped pair of sneakers shuffled by . . . Mr. Smith again. Jessie watched him go past. He was carrying one orange in a plastic bag.

Jessie thought about Mr. Smith while she ate her lunch. She wondered if he only had that one orange to eat for his lunch. She thought about his ragged coat and torn shoes. She couldn't get Mr. Smith out of her mind.

Suddenly she had an idea, "Grandma, I think I don't want anything for my birthday, okay? See, I was thinking . . . how about if you buy some shoes and shirts for Mr. Smith instead of getting presents for me?"

It looked like a tear was rolling down Grandma's cheek when she gave Jessie a big hug.

The Best Birthday Gift

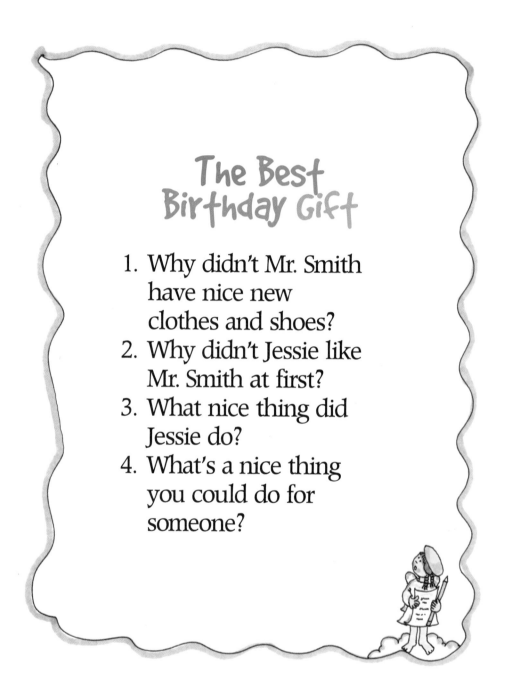

1. Why didn't Mr. Smith have nice new clothes and shoes?
2. Why didn't Jessie like Mr. Smith at first?
3. What nice thing did Jessie do?
4. What's a nice thing you could do for someone?

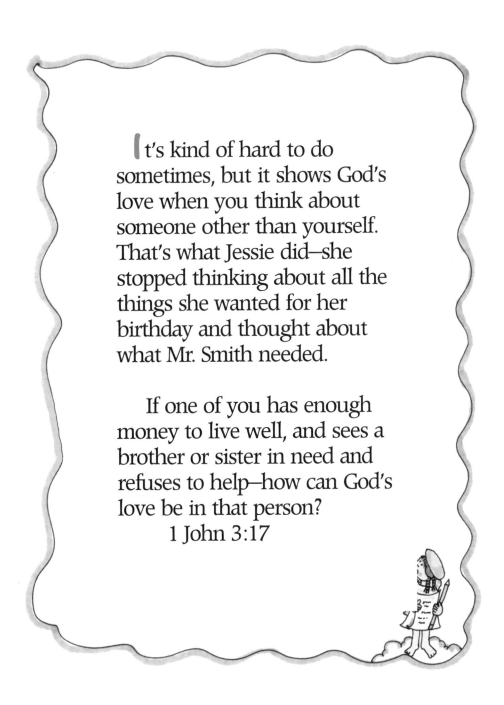

It's kind of hard to do sometimes, but it shows God's love when you think about someone other than yourself. That's what Jessie did—she stopped thinking about all the things she wanted for her birthday and thought about what Mr. Smith needed.

If one of you has enough money to live well, and sees a brother or sister in need and refuses to help—how can God's love be in that person?
1 John 3:17

The Best Me I Can Be!

"I wish I had yellow hair like Katie has. Yellow hair is prettier than stinky old brown hair," Christy moaned. Momma smiled and ruffled Christy's brown hair.

"I wish I didn't have freckles on my face.
Freckles are stinky," Christy sighed.
Momma kissed her finger and touched it
to the big freckle on the tip of Christy's nose.

...I wish I didn't have freckles....

"I wish I had blue eyes instead of brown ones," Christy said. "Brown eyes are stinky."

Momma just smiled at Christy with her own big brown eyes.

"I wish I could hit a softball like Megan does.
I'm not good at any sports," Christy pouted.
     Momma just smiled and dusted Christy's
gymnastics trophies.

"I wish I could play the piano like Sara does. I can't
do anything as good as she does," Christy whispered.
Momma didn't say anything. She just taped one
of Christy's very pretty paintings on the refrigerator.

"I wish I could . . ." Christy started to complain again. But, Momma shushed her. "Let's think of some good things about you," Momma suggested.

Christy wrinkled her nose and scratched her head. She couldn't think of anything to say. So, Momma helped her get started, "You sing so pretty and paint the most beautiful pictures. You are kind to people and gentle with babies and good with pets."

"I like to do gymnastics, and I like to read to my little brother. I'm good at helping you with chores, too," Christy was getting the idea now.

"Exactly! You are the best Christy ever, because God made you special! Want to know something else," Momma whispered, "God loves you just the way you are . . . and so do I!"

The Best Me
I Can Be

1. Why was Christy unhappy?
2. What are some good things Christy can do?
3. Do you ever wish you looked different or had different talents?
4. What are some good and kind things about you?

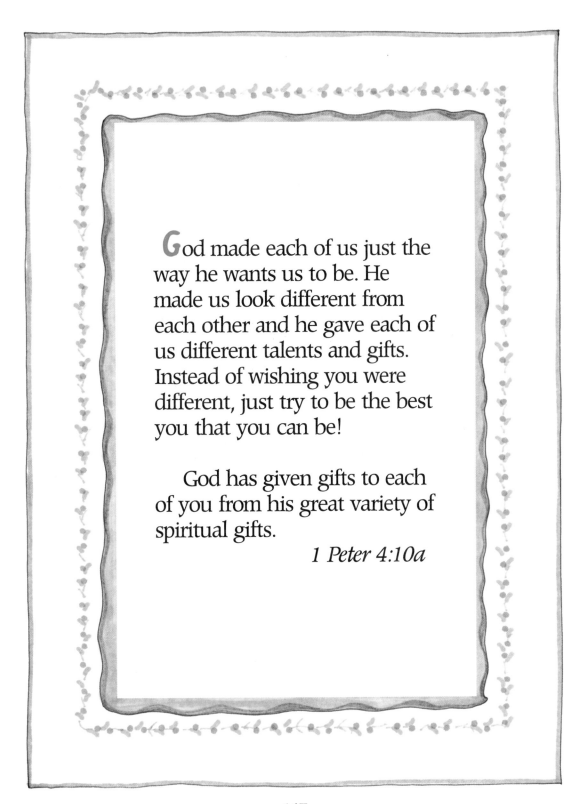

God made each of us just the way he wants us to be. He made us look different from each other and he gave each of us different talents and gifts. Instead of wishing you were different, just try to be the best you that you can be!

God has given gifts to each of you from his great variety of spiritual gifts.

1 Peter 4:10a

Prayers for Tammy

Alyssa sat on the front steps with her chin resting in her hands. She didn't feel like riding her bike or swinging or even eating a cookie. She was sad.

All Alyssa could think about was her friend, Tammy. They played together almost every day. They both liked to play school, draw pictures, and ride bikes. They were best friends.

But Tammy hadn't been able to play for a long
time, because she was sick—very sick. Alyssa
missed her very much. Every day she looked
at a big picture she had of Tammy and
wondered how her friend was feeling.

"What's the matter, Honey?" Momma sat down by Alyssa and handed her a fresh-baked cookie. Usually, Alyssa would eat a cookie right up. But, not today. Today all she could think about was Tammy.

"I'm scared, Momma. When is Tammy going to get well?" she whispered. "I miss playing with her and talking to her. I don't have anyone to make me laugh. And . . . I'm scared that she might die."

"We all want Tammy to get well," Momma said, giving Alyssa a hug. "The best thing we can do is pray for her and for the doctors to know how to take care of her."

"What if God doesn't listen to us?" Alyssa
wondered out loud.

"The Bible tells us that God hears all our
prayers. He wants to help us when we are scared
or sad. And the best thing is—he loves Tammy
even more than we do," Momma answered.

Alyssa thought about what Momma said. She thought about how much she loved Tammy and how much God must love her, too. Alyssa curled up on Momma's lap and together they asked God to take care of Tammy and help her get well soon.

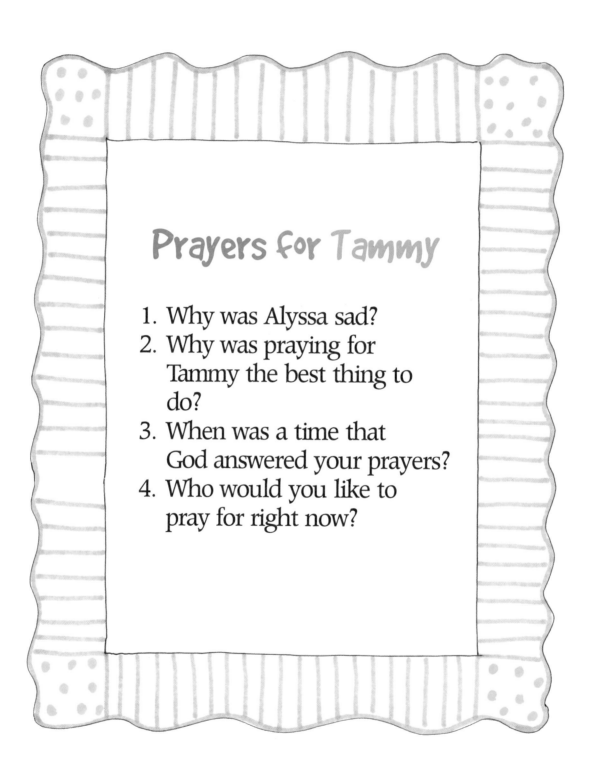

Prayers for Tammy

1. Why was Alyssa sad?
2. Why was praying for Tammy the best thing to do?
3. When was a time that God answered your prayers?
4. Who would you like to pray for right now?

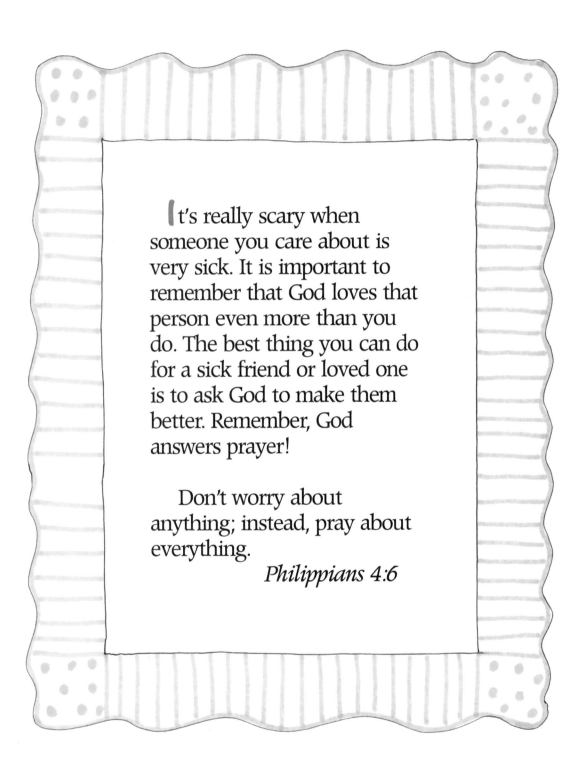

It's really scary when someone you care about is very sick. It is important to remember that God loves that person even more than you do. The best thing you can do for a sick friend or loved one is to ask God to make them better. Remember, God answers prayer!

Don't worry about anything; instead, pray about everything.

Philippians 4:6

My Mom

Some moms are tall.

Some moms are short.

Me and Mom

Some moms draw pretty pictures.

Some moms tell good stories.

Some moms are good at playing softball.

Some moms make good ooey-gooey-
chocolate-chip cookies.

Some moms sing funny songs and
wear silly hats.

But, of all the moms in the whole wide world,
God knew just what mom would be the very
best mom for me!

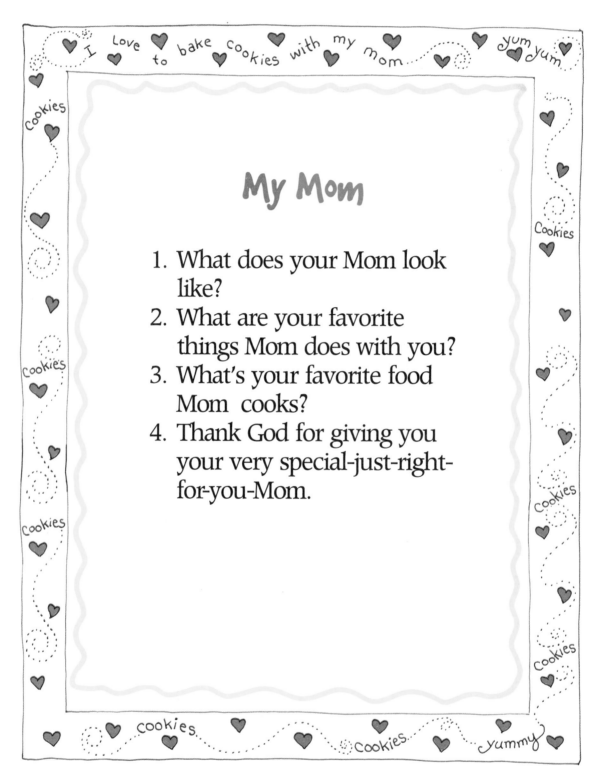

My Mom

1. What does your Mom look like?
2. What are your favorite things Mom does with you?
3. What's your favorite food Mom cooks?
4. Thank God for giving you your very special-just-right-for-you-Mom.

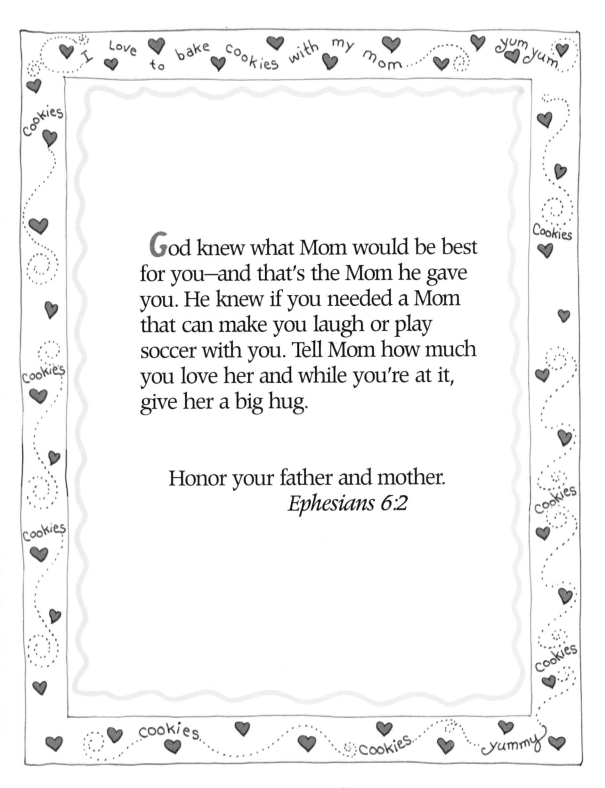

God knew what Mom would be best for you—and that's the Mom he gave you. He knew if you needed a Mom that can make you laugh or play soccer with you. Tell Mom how much you love her and while you're at it, give her a big hug.

Honor your father and mother.
Ephesians 6:2

167

The Broken Lamp

Hallie ran through the house, calling her dog, Digby to follow. Through the kitchen, the family room, around the corner to the dining room, across the living room, down the hallway and back to the kitchen.

168

Around and around Hallie ran as Digby chased her, yelping all the way. The third time through the living room, Hallie turned to look at Digby as she rounded a corner and she lost her balance and bumped a table.

Mom's favorite white lamp with pink roses on it
wiggled and wobbled and started falling to the floor. As
Hallie watched in horror, it seemed like it was falling in
slow motion. When it crashed to the floor in dozens of
pieces, Hallie knew she was in big trouble!

How many times had Mom said, "Don't run in the house, young lady." Hallie didn't want to think about it. She just stood and looked at the lamp pieces on the floor until she heard mom coming down the hallway.

"What happened here?" Mom asked quietly.

Hallie couldn't believe the words that came out of her mouth, "I was in the family room when I heard a crash. I guess Digby was running and he bumped the table," Hallie lied. Digby looked at her like he knew what she had just said.

"Digby, out you go," Momma said. She grabbed Digby's collar and pulled him to the door. "Digby will have to sleep on the back porch and stay outside from now on. He's too big to be in the house." Hallie looked through the window at Digby. He was looking back at her through the glass.

That night Hallie couldn't sleep. She missed
Digby sleeping by her bed. She was a little
scared without him there protecting her . . .
and she felt guilty for blaming him for the
broken lamp.

In the morning Hallie ran to Mom, "Please let Digby come back inside. He didn't break the lamp, I did!"

Mom took Hallie's face in her hands and looked deep into her eyes. "Hallie, why didn't you tell me the truth?"

"I guess I was scared—I know I'm not supposed to run in the house. I'm sorry I lied, Momma."

The Broken Lamp

1. What two things did Hallie do wrong?
2. Why did Hallie let Mom think Digby broke the lamp?
3. Have you ever told a lie to stay out of trouble?
4. How did you feel after you told the lie?

When you lie, it makes Mom feel she can't trust you anymore and that you don't care very much about her feelings. Lying never really solves a problem. You usually feel guilty about it; and sooner or later the person you lied to finds out about it. It's better to always tell the truth.

Don't lie to each other.
Colossians 3:9

The Right-Now Girl

"I want to go to Grandma's house," Becca shouted, pulling on Momma's arm.

"We'll go later, I have some things to do first," Momma answered.

"NO, RIGHT NOW!" Becca yelled.

"I want a cookie," Becca announced. She climbed from a chair to the counter and reached for the cookie jar.

"You can have one after lunch," Momma answered, scooting the cookie jar away.

"NO, RIGHT NOW!" Becca cried.

"I want to play with Mindy," Becca whined.

"First you need to have a rest time,"
Momma said.

"NO, RIGHT NOW!" Becca pouted.

"Buy me the new super-duper video game,"
Becca ordered.

"Maybe you'll get it for your birthday,"
Momma suggested.

"NO, RIGHT NOW!" Becca insisted.

"Play a game with me," Becca cried.

"I'll be happy to, as soon as I fold these towels," Momma said.

"NO, RIGHT NOW!" Becca shouted.

"Swing me at the park," Becca pulled on Momma's arm and said it again, "Let's go swing!"

"Just a minute. Let me finish making this food for dinner," Momma said.

"NO, RIGHT NOW!" Becca cried.

Let's go to the park!...

"Momma, read me a book!" Becca called, waving her favorite book in Momma's face.

"Sure, as soon as I change the baby's diaper," Momma smiled.

"NO, RIGHT NOW!" Becca shouted.

"Becca, my dear, you need to learn how to be patient," Momma said. "I love doing things with you, but I can't always drop what I'm doing. Patience means you wait for me to finish what I'm doing before I do something with you."

"OK," Becca said. "I will be more patient . . . RIGHT NOW!"

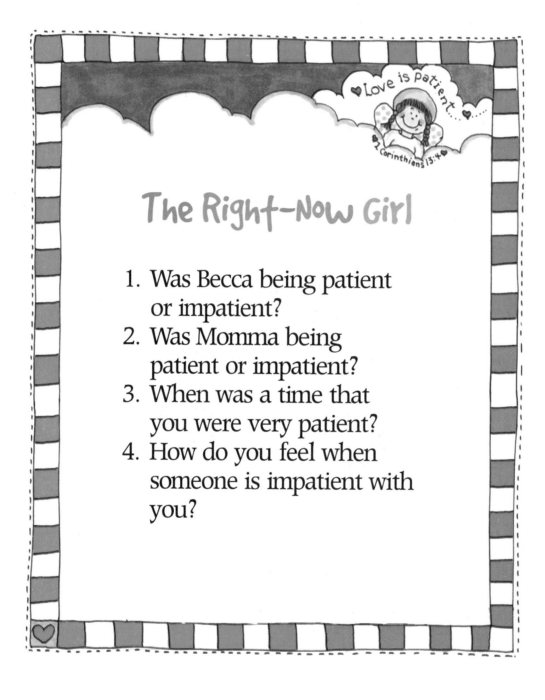

Love is patient...

2 Corinthians 13:4

The Right-Now Girl

1. Was Becca being patient or impatient?
2. Was Momma being patient or impatient?
3. When was a time that you were very patient?
4. How do you feel when someone is impatient with you?

Love is patient...
1 Corinthians 13:4

Being impatient and wanting to have your own way RIGHT NOW is very selfish. An impatient person doesn't care at all about how other people feel. Remember to think more about other people's feelings and less about your own.

Love is patient and kind.
1 Corinthians 13:4